reading babies

by
Danielle Dobbs

www.imagicprograms.com

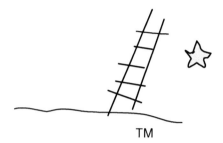

TM

I dedicate this book to our daughter, Rachelle,

from whom I have learned to experience the world

like never before and

have learned to find cuteness in a toad.

I must thank my husband and companion, Charles,

for his relentless support and optimism:

life is always "pretty good!"

WORKS
By
Danielle Dobbs

Reading Babies

Imagic Reading

The Imagical Power of Etymology

Reading Kit by Imagic - English
    140 Flashcards (black ink)

Reading And Language Kit by Imagic:
    English/Spanish -140 Flashcards (red and green)
    English/French - 140 Flashcards (red and blue)

Label books by Imagic:
    English Labels by Imagic
    Spanish Labels by Imagic
    French Labels by Imagic

The COPY-WRITE© Reading Kit –
    The Montessori method of teaching

TABLE OF CONTENTS

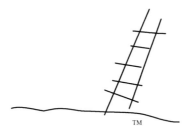

INTRODUCTION

The brain is a magical container that defies the laws of physics – the more you pour into it, the more it grows! The plasticity of the brain is directly related to its chronological age and the amount of stimulation it receives. The younger the child, the easier it is for the brain to meet the demands placed upon it. It is said that most of our learning is done within the first few years of life - by age three the circuitry of the brain is almost finished.

Anything having to do with languages seems to be an inborn ability, which includes learning to communicate in one or more languages, whether audible, or visible (sign language), and learning to read. It is during the early years that these tasks are best accomplished, when learning is pure fun!

As parents, we have big dreams for our children. After good health, our main goal is to ensure that they grow up to be happy and successful. We have a responsibility to help our children reach their full potential and take advantage of built in timing when everything is learned the easy way without the slightest effort. In so doing, our children will be given a brilliant start in life.

Teaching your baby to read is an act of love, because, unless you make a conscious effort to expose him to the printed word, he will not accomplish this task by himself. The techniques and material used to teach your baby to read are actually quite simple. However, it is your devotion to reading him stories and the interest you show that is of utmost importance in helping him develop a love for reading. With reading comes knowledge and with knowledge comes imagination.

Teaching him a second language will give him an edge in our competitive world while helping him develop respect and tolerance for other cultures. Your baby will easily learn to read and learn a second language because these activities are best acquired during the baby stage.

I have devoted a great portion of my book to giving tips for helping you meet the physical and psychological needs of your baby. Of all the many things you can give your baby, your time is the most precious. Talking to and listening to your baby will create a bond of friendship that will still endure during the teenage years and beyond. Confidence, good self-concept, a sense of security, a sense of fairness, a good sense of humor, and a love for the arts are traits worth nurturing in your child because all these will make him a well-rounded and well-adjusted person.

I have written *Reading Babies* because of my belief that every infant is endowed with an unlimited and magical learning potential. My intention is to share with you my success story about teaching our daughter to read while she was a baby and the ease with which she learned a second language, so that you too can help your child achieve his own learning potential.

Our daughter learned to read many words before she was able to speak. At one year old, she could read well over one hundred words printed on large flash cards while she was able to say only about 20 of these words. My husband and I read to her several books daily. Our motivation was to tell her enchanting stories. We did not concentrate on "teaching" her to read. Instead, we read her <u>stories</u>. Exposing her to words using flash cards from the time she was born gave her the idea that words were representations of real things, and printed words created stories. In so doing, she developed a true passion for reading. She had many toys but reading stories was her favorite activity.

At one year old, I decided to find out how much she could read by using a "guessing game" that I devised. We were amazed when, her bottle in hand, she walked through the 100 plus cards strewn on the floor of the living room picking out correctly any word I asked her. This is how we knew she could read. Besides using large flash cards, I had also labeled things around the house with 3x5 cards because of my conviction that babies can learn to read by association.

We never asked her to read, and it is only by chance that we learned that, at three years of age, she could fluently read entire books. One night, as usual, she carried a pile of books to bed that we had borrowed from the library a few hours before. Since I was sick with fever I told her I would read only <u>one</u> book. After finishing the book I reminded her that, as always, I would read her many books the next day. After her plea did not change my mind, she picked up the next (new) book from the top of the pile and read, out loud, the entire book. Her attitude seemed to say "See, I don't need you, I can do it by myself!" My fever magically disappeared as I called my husband to witness the event. Amazingly, as her little finger glided on the page, her reading was fluent with the right voice inflection.

Soon after, she started taking Suzuki violin lessons, but she did not like to practice. So I devised a game, which I called "Treasure Hunt." I hid either a cookie or a candy somewhere in the house. I wrote a set of instructions on a piece of paper and handed it to her after she finished practicing her violin. Her reward was to go on a treasure hunt and find the "loot." This rewarding game worked like magic - she practiced her violin with anticipation of her reward.

One night, I found out how much this game meant to her. While she was practicing, I was preparing our luggage to leave the next day for France to visit my father. Since I had much to do, I handed her a cookie after she had finished practicing her violin and praised her for how well she did. She burst out crying in disappointment, "Oh no, Maman, the treasure hunt!" You can imagine how bad I felt. I, of course, had to oblige and devise another set of instructions and hide the cookie.

At 4 years old, while on a trip to France to visit my father, she amazed us once again. She was bilingual, English-French, but she only had a few French books at home, and she read mostly books in English. I told her that night that I would be reading the French books we had borrowed a few days before from the library. I had been so busy with my father that I had failed to read these books to her. She answered that she had read them. I said (in French) "You mean you looked at the pictures?" She replied (as a matter of fact, as if it was no big deal) "No, I've read them." We gave her the books and asked her to show us. She read them fluently! Her love of reading had motivated her to decipher the French text all by herself, and there is no telling how long she had been able to read in French.

Her case is not unusual. Many babies achieve the same results given the same opportunity we gave our daughter. The idea of teaching babies to read does not seem so far-fetched when one considers that ALL babies learn to talk within the first few years of life and this is far more difficult than having to recognize some words that spring out of books in enchanting stories.

Our baby has now grown to be a happy young lady who, at nineteen, will soon be graduating with a Bachelor's degree in Chemistry with plans to go to graduate school. She is a well-rounded person who not only loves science and computers, but also loves the arts. We cherish the fact that she is very close to us both. We wish every parent the joy of parenthood and a good journey together with your child.

Note to parents: *Throughout my book, I have referred to baby as "he." I felt it awkward to be politically correct by having to say "he/she" or "his/her." Since I am a practical person, I consider "baby" and "he" to include both genders. The same is true regarding parents, no need to say Mama Bear or Papa Bear.*

TIMING AND READING

The clock is ticking. In human evolution, the concept of timing in children's development has been reduced to stages involving mainly physical skills such as crawling, walking, and potty training. The "terrible twos" also take center stage and new parents are warned ahead of time to brace themselves as if this stage was utterly unavoidable. From the grunts of cave men to our more sophisticated mode of communication, babies have been able to imitate, learn, and assimilate complex language skills. We have taken this amazing feat for granted and accepted this activity as simply what babies do.

Let's stop and think for a moment and marvel at the unbelievable task of a baby learning a language. ALL babies learn to understand their language <u>before</u> they are able to control their speech. With practice, in the span of three years, they achieve the unthinkable - they are able to use a complex language skill, in which a string of words has been arranged into complete sentences. And, this ladies and gentlemen is an absolute tour de force. Imagine the amount of learning that took place within those few years. In our failure to marvel at this feat of nature, we have failed to ask ourselves:

What else could babies do?

Several hundred years ago, the main focus of early schools was to teach reading, writing and arithmetic to young children six years of age or older. One can surmise that the age at which they started school had probably been chosen because children's fine motor skills are better developed around that age. Since they can control the pencil and learn to write by copying a printed word, reading and writing became inseparable activities. However, the question is:

Could reading be taught much earlier, before fine motor skills?

Yes, indeed! I firmly believe that reading and writing should be disassociated so that reading is taught to babies during language development and writing taught later when fine motor skills are better developed.

In modern times, pre-schools and nurseries were instituted to give mothers a chance to work outside the home. Because of this, the prevalent attitude arose that attending pre-school was necessary to give Johnny a head start so he could learn his ABC's. In the process, parents began to think that school was the place where all learning began, and teachers knew best how to teach our children. WRONG!

Most of the learning takes place <u>before</u> Johnny starts school. It is a fact that as the brain grows, it becomes less plastic and willing to learn new tricks. Knowing this, shouldn't we start revising our thinking toward schools and most of all, change our attitude toward learning in general?

There is no doubt that schoolteachers are invaluable assets to our society, but aren't we discounting ourselves? Parents are "born teachers" - we teach our children naturally and instinctively. We teach and reinforce a highly complex language in our children from the time they are born and we are quite successful because ALL our children learn to speak their native language during the first few years of life.

6

Parents of all nationalities have an innate ability to teach their baby to speak. This teaching takes on the form of question and answer - "What is …?" and "It is …" We instinctively speak slowly and distinctly to our baby and repeat the sentence several times to emphasize a particular word.

"Look at the dog!"
"What is that?"
"Is that a dog?"
"Yes, that's a dog!"
"A dog!"
"Isn't that a nice dog!"

Since varied sentence structure, with repetition of essential elements, is the key to learning, it is clear that the above monologue shows that we are endowed with a natural ability to teach, and we do it without having been taught! We have been repetitive without being boring.

In the life cycle of living things, timing can be viewed as definite events occurring at definite times according to various biological clocks in a species. This clock is pre-programmed, so to speak, so that a particular skill is best acquired during a certain period. I want to stress "acquired" because the essence of timing means that learning a particular task is easier during a certain period, and consequently it would be more difficult if it took place at any other time. In the animal world, timing means survival, which involves primarily getting the baby to the mature stage as quickly as possible so that it can take care of itself. In contrast, we nurture our babies until they go to college. Our world is naturally very complex, but it seems that we are not taking full advantage of our built-in, pre-programmed clock.

In recent years, interesting studies have been done on inborn timing and swimming. It was found that there is a small window of time, from birth to about six months, during which a baby can learn to swim without fear. They instinctively paddle, turn on their back and float. Past six months, babies panic and drown. We need to ask the questions:

What are the innate abilities of babies?

and

What else can they do besides learning their native language, walking and swimming?

If we look at the head size of an infant compared to his little body, this should give us a clue as to its importance. It is during this stage, when the brain is still plastic, that it can make complex neurological connections. Their enormous relative brain size would suggest that babies are designed to perform as much brain activity as possible during the baby stage.

HOW A BABY LEARNS

When babies learn to speak, they verbalize sound patterns to represent a concrete thing or a concept. With the help of his senses, the baby will learn about the world around him. Let's take "water" for example.

A baby will have to learn and cross-reference between his senses that all of the following mean "water.

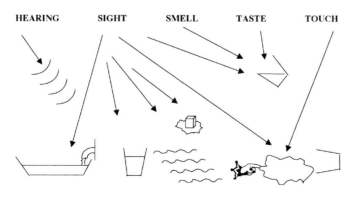

HEARING   SIGHT   SMELL   TASTE   TOUCH

9

What if the baby was shown one more piece of information, namely the word "WATER?" Some may argue that the written word is simply a representation of water and thus might be more difficult for the child to grasp. What about the following:

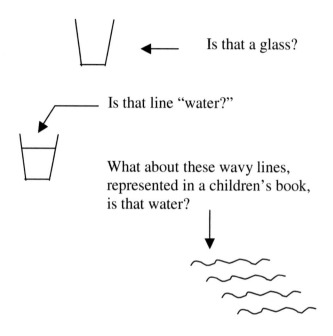

The baby is taught that the above wavy lines represent water, just as he is supposed to assume that the line inside the glass represents "water."

The squiggly lines in "WATER" we call a "written word" are not that different in terms of representing the concept of "WATER," than the wavy lines above. A baby will not ask any questions about the above, he'll just take your word for it.

Is that a glass of water? Not really, but we convince ourselves it is, and we teach our babies that it is.

So, let's add the word "WATER" to the <u>concept</u> of water.

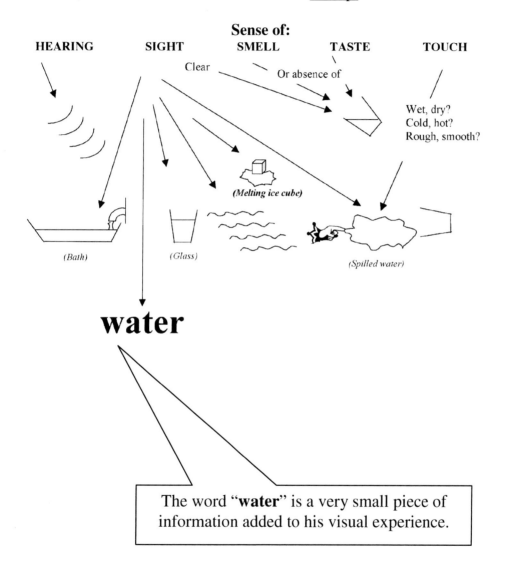

Sense of:

HEARING   SIGHT   SMELL   TASTE   TOUCH

Clear   Or absence of

Wet, dry?
Cold, hot?
Rough, smooth?

(Melting ice cube)

(Bath)   *(Glass)*   *(Spilled water)*

water

The word "**water**" is a very small piece of information added to his visual experience.

As the child learns more and more about the properties of water - wet, clear, lack of smell, liquid, can spill, different temperatures, it is quite easy to learn that WATER can also be called "EAU" or "AGUA." This is no big deal for a child. His brain is plastic and anything that comes to his mind finds a place, is catalogued and is cross-referenced with ease.

Sense of:

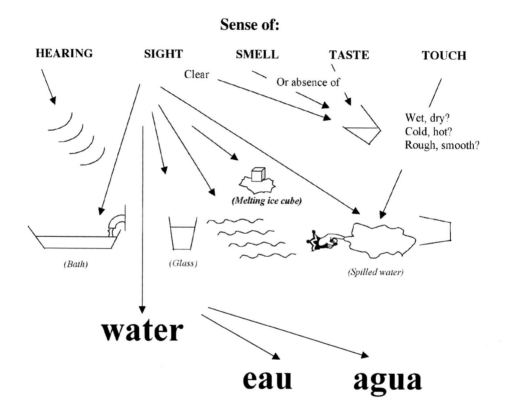

The baby learns a tremendous amount of information through all his senses. The printed word is just another visual piece of information and he does not need to verbalize anything.

When learning to read, the squiggle representation of the word WATER is picked up by the eyes, then the image is sent to the brain and the association is made with the concept of water. During this process, the word is physically there on the printed page; while sound, on the other hand, disappears as it reaches the ear, and there is no possibility of recheck. Once the words have been learned, the process of reading involves only word recognition, which is an easier process than the process of recalling a sound and attempting to repeat it.

The process involved in learning to talk is much more complex than learning to read. Besides having to recall the exact pronunciation, speaking involves a multi-layer physical activity of the larynx, lungs, tongue, lips (and teeth.) In learning to speak, waves of different amplitudes reach the ear, and impulses are sent electrically to the brain where they are interpreted. The association between sound and actual water will be made way before the baby is physically able to speak. He will then imitate and try to vocalize the word. For this he needs to recall how it sounds, then he will try to match his vocal attempts to something that resembles the pronunciation of "water."

One can deduct that, from the baby's point of view, learning to read must be an easier task compared to learning to speak because reading is a passive activity while speaking requires much effort. Thus, it is my belief that if children can achieve the formidable task of learning to speak by age three, then they could be reading by that age.

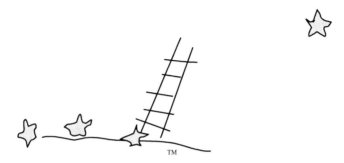

THE FUTURE OF EDUCATION

Reading is the fundamental basis of education. All other subjects taught in school depend upon the art of reading. If by kindergarten a child is not a reader it is doubtful that he will later develop a love of reading. It is time we give ALL children a brilliant start in life – and this depends primarily on us, the parents.

I must argue with the skeptics that if monkeys by age three, then our babies can certainly match their performance. Researchers working with chimpanzees have documented the amazing ability of chimps to learn "human tasks." Now, chimpanzees cannot only learn to communicate with humans using sign language, they can also be taught to read. Researchers at Kyoto University in Japan have been successful in teaching a 25-year-old chimpanzee to read several dozen Japanese kanji characters – a form of Japanese writing. Ai, as she is called, using a computer, learned to match written words to colors and objects. One day, researchers were shocked when they saw Ai's 10-month-old son, Ayumu, quickly go to the monitor and match the word for brown with the brown square. "It was astonishing!" said Tersuro Matsuzawa, a primatologist at the university, because Ayumu had taught himself to read without any coaching by <u>simply</u> <u>watching</u> <u>his</u> <u>mother</u>.

Closer to home, Dr. Sally Boysen, Psychologist from the Ohio State University Chimpanzee Center has documented her extensive work with chimps, specifically with Keeli and Ivy, two chimps who were taught to read with the use of a computer screen. Boysen recorded their incredible ability to match whole words with real objects and pictures. Boysen remarks that chimps are very similar to us in that they also possess an understanding of concepts and they can be trained to name objects and even name other chimps by matching their proper names to their pictures.

One can learn about the prowess of chimps in research journals or newspapers, but what about publicizing the learning potential of our babies? Newspapers devote pages on the failure of our educational system and reporters continue to berate the growing concerns of educators to reach the goal of teaching children to read by nine! Many "remedial" reading programs are implemented which give poor results. It is time for the media to report positive news and inform the public about a new approach to education. The ability to read is innate, which can be developed at the same time babies acquire their native language - this novel approach would give children a brilliant start in life.

However, this "novel" approach is not new and has been around for over 20 years. Glenn Doman, a renowned human developmentalist and a pioneer in teaching babies to read, has given lectures all over the world about the learning potential of "tiny children." What is most remarkable is that he has helped children with Down syndrome and others to reach their full potential. It seems that the younger the children are when they start his program, the better the results. In his book *How To Teach Your Baby To Read*, he reports that he, his wife, and staff have even been successful in teaching reading to brain damaged children.

The experience I have gained on a day-to-day basis, teaching reading and French to our daughter has been invaluable because I was able to observe and take note of her progress. Since I was also teaching French to babies and toddlers, I was able to record the progress of my little students according to their ages. I came to the conclusion that the best time to teach those skills is during the preverbal years. It is during that time that their aptitude to master these tasks is at its peak!

Masaru Ibuka, author of *Kindergarten Is Too Late*, stresses that we need to give children a learning opportunity at a very young age. Consequently the educational idea of teaching basic skills to children in kindergarten will be a thing of the past and our educational system will improve.

No one can do the job but parents. We must take charge to help our children reach their inborn potential by giving them the opportunities they deserve. We already do a fantastic job in teaching them their native language, so we can certainly teach them how to read as well. Parents and educators need to take a good look at why 10 year old Johnny can't read. All children, including Johnny, are born with the capability for brilliance. The question remains - what has caused Johnny to underachieve?

It is time to drop the traditional view of education and look at current programs such as *Born To Read – Florida Style*, a project sponsored by the Florida Department of State and funded by the Federal Library Services and Technology Act. Various state programs like this are invaluable because government officials are now recognizing the importance of infant stimulation and encouraging parents to expose their babies to books. With the partnership of librarians, health care providers and community service organizations, these programs are designed to raise the awareness of new parents in their children's abilities to read, with the goal of instilling a love of reading in their babies.

In all fairness schoolteachers are there to teach, not to accomplish miracles with children who have not received proper nurturing during their early years. Parents must start exposing their babies to the printed word and read them stories on a daily basis so that their children will be reading way before kindergarten. These children will pick up books to read not because

17

they are told to "read a book" but because they <u>want</u> to read and have fun.

In recent times, progress has been made in schools with regards to implementing accelerated classes to meet the needs of the gifted. These children have been recognized as having "special needs" because they seem to surpass average children on qualifying tests. Could it be that these children are really the norm and that the "average" children are actually behind?

Let us reflect on modern times for a moment. We have, to name a few things, computers, the internet, radio, instant news from around the world, TV, video and audiocassettes, CDs, newspapers, magazines, the ability to visit almost any place, and man can go into space and come back. Today children are bombarded with much more information than children living one hundred years ago. Yet, our basic education system has not really changed. We can imagine that a 4-year old today is much "smarter" and aware of his world around him than a 4-year old child living 100 years ago on the farm and having one book at home – the Bible. With so much information and the availability of books of all kinds, our children should be geniuses!

The sonic boom of our information age should wake us up to a new age in education. The bar must be raised and our expectations of student performance increased. To start, we must stop talking about "the 3Rs" - Reading, Riting, and Rithmetic. How competent are we to talk about education when we confuse our children with Reading "Riting" and "Rithmetic." Secondly, reading and writing should be disassociated so that reading is taught at the time of language development and writing taught later when the child has gained fine motor control. By kindergarten children should be expected to read fluently. From then on schoolchildren would be challenged intellectually. The teacher could discuss and draw lessons from stories the students read in their books the night before; or discuss other subjects rather than drilling the children in phonics, which is boring and unexciting. This would make school an exciting place, from the lower grades to high school.

TM

TIMING AND A SECOND LANGUAGE

At one time, learning a second language was reserved for nobles or diplomats. Since learning a foreign language was (and is still) not an easy task for adults, it was thought that it would be even harder for a child. Wrong! Some of us have experienced meeting a new family of immigrants. Six months later, the children speak fluent English while the parents are still struggling with the basics.

Language development occurs naturally, in a timely fashion. Anyone learning a foreign language as an adult cannot help but wonder how they were able to learn their own language so easily. The answer is timing.

**Language development occurs naturally and easily
during the infant and toddler stages
and it is during these stage that multiple languages should be taught.**

* * *

Today's growing awareness of the global marketplace and the ease with which we travel from country to country, emphasize the need for teaching foreign languages.

The idea of teaching foreign languages is good but the timing is **<u>awful!</u>** Presently, most foreign language programs are introduced in high school and college and are imposed as a requirement for graduation. Valuable time and effort are being wasted by students trying to memorize lessons and to acquire proper pronunciation. Too often the student can pass a written foreign language course without being required to verbalize anything.

Educators must realize that the teaching of a foreign language after the early years is an unnatural phenomenon, and it is met by our natural resistance to learning "gibberish" in grammatical form. Instead, foreign languages should be introduced to children at an early age at the time they learn their native language. Young children learn to communicate in any language they become exposed to, while, at the same time, acquiring the proper pronunciation. Their brain is magical - it does all the work unconsciously.

* * *

Babies have an amazing talent for picking up meaning from the gibberish they hear around them. The tone and inflection of our voice conveys images to others, even without the proper words. Read the following poem and see what pictures and feelings you get, despite the fact that Lewis Carroll has not used many intelligible words. To our surprise we get the pictures as well as the emotions associated with the sounds.

The Jabberwocky

Twas brillig, and the slithy toves
Did gyre and gimble in the wabe:
All mimsy were the borogoves,
And the mome raths outgrabe.

"Beware the Jabberwock, my son!
The jaws that bite, the claws that catch!
Beware the Jubjub bird, and shun
The frumious Bandersnatch!"

He took his vorpal sword in hand:
Long time the manxome foe he sought—
So rested he by the Tumtum tree,
And stood awhile in thought.

And, as in uffish thought he stood,
The Jabberwock, with eyes of flame,
Came whiffling through the tulgey wood,
And burbled as it came!

One, two! One, two! And through and through
The vorpal blade went snicker-snack!
He left it dead, and with its head
He went galumphing back.

"And hast thou slain the Jabberwock?
Come to my arm, my beamish boy!
O frabjous day! Callooh! Callay!"
He chortled in his joy.

'Twas brillig, and the slithy toves
Did gyre and gimble in the wabe:
All mimsy were the borogoves,
And the mome raths outgrabe

(Carroll, *The Annotated Alice*, 191-97)

Leonard Bernstein, famous conductor and composer spoke several languages fluently. He once discussed the relationship of language and music. He explained that certain words in various languages possess similar musical tone such as Maman, Mommy and Mutter - they all have the sound of "mm" which evoke something soothing and comforting. He was also making a point that music speaks to us by invoking various emotions.

Language is music and each language has its own melody and rhythm. Young children have the ability to learn several languages at the same time and not get confused because it is as if each language had its own song. Parents need to be reassured that children will not get "confused." In fact, children know exactly what language is being spoken and they will not mix-up sounds. Once, our 3-year-old little girl pointed to a fire hydrant while we were going on a stroll. We were talking in French and she asked me what it was. Forgetting the word in French, I said "C'est un fire hydrant!" She then said, "Mais, non, qu'est-ce que c'est en français?" – But, no, what is it in French? The sound of "fire hydrant" did not fit into the French (lyrical) melody.

A study on "Language Discrimination by Newborns," published in the *Journal of Experimental Psychology Human and Perception and Performance* in June of 1998, reveals that newborns use "rhythmic information" in order to classify speech according to global rhythmic patterns. Since each language has its own cadence, this implies that babies can classify and differentiate between languages.

In his book *Our Kind*, Marvin Harris found that there are less than 50 distinct sounds that are used to build words and sentences. The interesting thing is that infants produce a wider variety of vocalizations than adults, but with time, they select only the sound needed to produce their language. The implication is that babies raised in a bilingual environment will widen their range of sounds to include the pitch of that second language.

In her research on pitch, Diane Deutsch of the University of California has found that each culture has a definite speech range. She found that the speech range of Vietnamese starts and ends at about E, while the pitch range exhibited by Californians have a range that starts and ends at C sharp.

Another incredible thing is that the brain of a young child is able to deduce grammar! Once, our 3-year-old little girl was very excited with a new toy that drew shapes. She excitedly came to me and said "Maman, tu veux … tu veux … tu veux …" (You want . . .) In her excitement she could not think of the word in French, so she finally blurted "Tu veux tryer?" (You want to try?) I was dumfounded! She took the verb "to try" and added the French infinitive "er" to "try." Her brain knew the corresponding verb in English and in a split second she proceeded to add the French infinitive "er" to "try" to what seemed like a good candidate as a root word. The correct sentence in French being "Tu veux essayer?".

Young children learn languages in a different fashion than adults. They learn a language at the <u>unconscious level</u> while adults have to be very active in learning it at the <u>conscious level</u>. Young children mimic and learn "<u>sound patterns.</u>" Adults learn how to put together some memorized conjugation in a grammatical sentence and attempt to pronounce the whole thing in an enthusiastic way with a foreign accent! To those people, I tip my hat. It can certainly be done, but it is not an easy task.

Children take everything in without questioning anything. They learn an entire sentence describing an action just as if that entire sentence was a synonym in their native language. Joy Hirsch, a neuroscientist, and her colleagues from the Memorial Sloan-Kettering Cancer Institute Center in New York found that bilingual individuals who had acquired a second language during infancy showed the same increased neuronal activity in the same part of the brain as the place for their native language. On the other hand, individuals who acquired their second language as adults showed neuronal activity in a different part of the brain. This presents an interesting point. The fact that memorization of a second language by an adult takes place in a different part of the brain, could imply that everything about the second language is stand-alone material. In contrast, bilingual children might benefit from an adjacent corresponding "cross reference" library, as both languages are stored in the same part of the brain, thus giving the infant an advantage on connecting the two languages.

All the children I have observed who have been raised in a bilingual environment have no problem switching back and forth between the two languages. They seem to take a whole sound pattern as a synonym of a corresponding idea in their other language. "J'ai soif" becomes another way of saying "I'm thirsty." They will learn "Jaisoif" (Iamthirsty), "Jaifaim" (Iamhungry), "Jenaipassoif" (Iamnothungry) as a whole sound pattern. Their brains arrange and chop up those sounds according to some logical grammatical pattern. This is done on the unconscious level. As they age, they loose the ability to absorb and "take everything in."

To illustrate this, I once knew a French couple who had been transferred from Paris to Denver. They enrolled their 4-year-old son in a pre-school. One week later, the mother asked her little boy in near to perfect English "What are you doing?" The little boy looked at her with a blank look and asked her in French what she was saying. The mother explained in French. The little boy told her that she was WRONG ... because his friends say "whachyadoin'!"

As adults, we have become too rational. We want to learn bite-size "words" because we fear we would get "confused" (and we would) if we were to learn an entire sentence based only upon phonetics. We need to chop up, analyze, make sure words are spelled correctly, pronounced correctly, and only then do we "consciously" put it in our brain with grammatical epithets such as "nouns," adjectives," "verbs," etc. Learning a language is a natural phenomenon for children. For us, it's WORK! Seeing all the things we must do to input and store it in our brains, it is indeed WORK!

It is a fact that children learn languages with ease. They learn extremely fast, but they forget just as fast if they are no longer exposed to a particular language. Once I knew a 2 1/2-year old British girl who spent twenty days in France at her grandparents' house while her parents visited France. Her father was French, her mother British. When they returned to England, where I was living at the time, she had forgotten how to speak English but I could speak and converse with her in French. Several weeks later, her English had come back and she could then converse in French with her father and in English with her mother. For this reason, it is important that

24

once a language has been acquired that children continue to be exposed to that language, or at the very least, continue to hear it with audio and video cassettes; otherwise, they will forget very quickly.

By the age of 4 or 5, after a child has acquired an extensive vocabulary, introducing another language can be a very frustrating experience for him. Now, he loses the control he has had of his environment and he may at first resist learning "a new song." This is why teaching a child a second language before they develop an extensive vocabulary is of vital importance. A baby will know instinctively that a different language is being spoken to him because it has a different melody and rhythm. He will learn quickly that to communicate with the Spanish baby sitter, he will have to talk in a particular way and with his parents talk another way. Being consistent is the key.

When parents move to a foreign country with their children and they are immersed into a new language, the child learns to communicate quickly, faster than his parents. The original frustration is replaced by his heightened desire to play and communicate with kids his age and he will practice the language by imitating his friends without asking any questions.

By exposing children to foreign languages while they acquire their native language, children will develop tolerance and respect for other cultures. In addition, they will learn the customs and culture of the respective country, which is woven into the language. With growing international trade, foreign languages are a must to compete in a global market.

The teaching of foreign languages should start at home, in nurseries, daycare and at the latest, pre-school, definitely not in high schools or universities. Very young children need to be taught now, otherwise, we are wasting a valuable potential, which, by remaining untapped, will be lost within a few years. Timing is of the essence. The best time to teach a language is during the pre-verbal stage.

I have taught French to very young children and have found that the younger they are at the time they are exposed to a second language, the easier and faster they learn. My experience has shown me that all children possess the ability to learn multiple languages. Making sounds and mimicking seems to be an inborn ability and pastime.

TM

GIFTED CHILDREN AND IQ

All children are born with the capacity for brilliance. In this sense, they are born gifted. It is up to us to help them reach their full potential. All children are curious and possess an insatiable desire to discover and learn about things around them. Some children have some physical limitations, but considering that we only use a very small amount of our brain, there are plenty of neurons sitting around that could be trained or retrained to learn a task. Glenn Doman, who wrote *What to Do About Your Brain-Injured Child*, has worked extensively with brain-damaged children and he has shown that they too can learn to read.

Every so-called "gifted child" has a gifted parent. In his brilliant book *How To Be A Gifted Parent*, David Lewis, the world famous British psychologist and writer, lists 40 statements that describe the traits of gifted parents. He suggests that parents take the following test and respond to each statement.

1. I answer all questions from my child as patiently and honestly as possible.

2. I take serious questions or statements from my child seriously.

3. I provide a bulletin board where my child can show off his/her work.

4. I am prepared to tolerate an untidy work area if my child has not yet completed some creative task (i.e., painting, model making, etc.).

5. I provide my child with a room or part of the room, exclusively for his/her own use.

6.

6. I show my child he/she is loved for his/her own sake, not for achievements.

7. I give my child responsibilities suitable to his/her age.

8. I help him/her make his/her *own* plans and decisions.

9. I take my child on trips to places of interest.

10. I teach my child how to improve on the task he/she does.

11. I encourage my child to get along with children from different backgrounds.

12. I set a reasonable standard of behavior and see that my child follows it.

13. I never compare my child unfavorably to other children.

14. I never denigrate my child as a form of punishment.

15. I provide hobby materials and books.

16. I encourage my child to think things out for himself/herself.

17. I read regularly to my child.

18. I teach my child early reading habits.

19. I encourage my child to invent stories and fantasies.

20. I give careful consideration to the individual needs of each child.

21. I provide a time each day when my child can be alone with me.

22. I allow my child to have a say in making family plans or trips.

23. I never mock my child for making a mistake.

24. I encourage my child to remember stories, poems, and songs.

25. I encourage my child to be sociable with adults of all ages.

26. I devise practical experiments to help my child find out about things.

27. I allow my child to play with all kinds of junk objects.

28. I encourage my child to look for problems and then solve them.

29. I look for specific things to praise in my child's activities.

30. I avoid general praise, which I do not really mean.

31. I am honest about my emotions with my child.

32. I do not have any subjects, which I would totally refuse to discuss with my child.

33. I provide opportunities for real decision making by my child.

34. I encourage my child to be an individual.

35. I help my child find worthwhile programs on TV.

36. I encourage my child to think positively about his/her abilities.

37. I never dismiss failures by my child with the comment: "I can't do it either!"

38. I encourage my child to be as independent of adults as possible.

39. I have faith in my child's good sense and trust him/her.

40. I would sooner my child failed by himself/herself than succeeded because I did most of the work.

He recommends that you score yourself by adding all the check marks and if you can answer a statement as something you do frequently but not all the time, then give yourself 1/2 point.

Gifted parents in his study scored 30 points and above. If you scored less than that, he suggests that you try to incorporate some of these activities into your daily routine.

Lewis lists four attributes pertinent to the gifted child, but he points out that the first attribute, the amount of confidence, is the most important one of all:
   a) The amount of confidence with which the child undertakes an unfamiliar task,
   b) The span of attention he displays in solving problems,
   c) His self-image,
   d) The way that he is regarded by adults.

All babies seem to display an incredible amount of confidence in everything they undertake. Whether they will maintain their high degree of confidence is mainly due to parental influence. If parents continually rebuke the child's efforts to explore and learn about his environment by saying "No, don't do this!" "No, you can't do that!" it is easy to foresee that the child's confidence will be diminished and, as he grows up, a "can't do" attitude will prevail. Therefore, it is important to avoid having to say "no" by putting the baby in a safe situation where he will be allowed and encouraged to explore at will.

There is no doubt that proper nutrition plays a great part in the development of the brain - during gestation and after the child is born. Thus the importance of the mother getting adequate nourishment during pregnancy. Nature is so well designed that it gave babies an insurance policy by making sure that the baby will receive all it needs from the mother's milk. Research shows that babies who are breastfed develop higher IQs because certain chemicals in breast milk help the baby's brain develop.

Early stimulation involving audible, visual and tactile experiences do increase children's IQs. Recently, with the help of the media, a little progress has been achieved in disseminating research that shows that exposing babies and toddlers to music improves their IQs. As a result, many nurseries are now playing Mozart for babies with the hope of improving their intelligence.

However, some researchers dispute these benefits and claim that exposure to music makes no difference in IQ. I personally feel that any stimulation is good and music can only add to the child's listening and learning experience.

Recently, research conducted by Diana Deutsch at the University of California in San Diego revealed that perfect pitch can be learned, but only in infancy. She postulates that the learning may even start in the womb. "The noise of the mother's voice comes through very loudly during pregnancy," says Deutsch. She also suggests parents expose young children to musical instruments on which notes are labeled.

31

In our case, my husband is tone deaf and I do not play any instruments. But, when our daughter was a baby I played a lot of classical music. In addition, I used to sing the musical scale: do, ré, mi, fa, sol, la, ti, do. Later, when she started violin at age three, we discovered that she had perfect pitch.

Bilingual children seem to develop higher IQs. Research done in Canada with French-English students show that bilingual students performed better on tests than monolingual students.

Children who communicate early seem to develop a larger vocabulary and a higher IQ. In his book *The Einstein Syndrome*, Thomas Sowell states that as a rule early talking and early reading are reliable signs of high IQ. However, Sowell cautions that this is not always the case. He points out that Einstein was a late talking child and he was thought to be "subnormal."

Another form of communication that increases IQ is teaching babies to sign during the pre-verbal stage. Researchers have found that as a group, children who learned to sign as babies had a mean IQ of 114 compared to 102 of non-signers. Deaf parents report that it is common for their babies, deaf or hearing, to communicate in sign as early as six months old. This means that, even though the verbal skills are not yet developed, babies communicate on a higher level with their deaf parents beyond the usual cooing and body language. Imagine the feeling of security and confidence babies must get when they are able to communicate their needs as they arise. Babies no longer have to wait for their parents to guess what they need.

When our baby girl was growing up, we thought that she was the norm and all the other children her age were behind. It had never occurred to us that she was ahead until at 3 1/2 years old she was tested to get into a pilot program run by a local university. We were told that she tested well above average. We really feel that her score was due, in great part, to her ability to read fluently and being bilingual.

Children with higher IQs go well beyond usual expectations. One time, I enrolled our daughter at the Botanical Gardens in Denver. The class was designed for 5 year olds. She was barely four at the time but since she was tall,

I figured no one would be asking any questions. Two hours later, parents came to pick up their children, and like them, I was waiting at the door. I observed that all the children were sitting at a round table. In the middle of the table was a cactus, and next to it was a ball of clay with toothpicks poked in it. Every child had his ball of clay and each was meticulously putting toothpicks into the clay. I observed the teacher going around the table and complimenting each child. When she came to our daughter, she looked then she skipped her.

Now, I was very puzzled as to why she had not complimented my daughter like the other kids. Our daughter seemed very preoccupied with her project. From where I was I could not see her work but I could see that from time to time she would stand and press something on the table. The teacher informed parents that we could come in. I saw my daughter pressing her piece of clay into something flat as a pancake. She said, "Look, Maman, my cactus!" My reply, "Um very nice, but I think you are supposed to put toothpicks in it." She replied, "Oh, but I have some toothpicks . . . " then she lowered her voice as if it was something secretive, she said " . . . but they are inside!" She lifted her "pancake" a bit to show me, and I could see some toothpicks embedded in it. I said "Um, why did you do that?" She replied, "Because this way, animals won't hurt themselves!" I was dumbfounded!

Since our daughter is an animal lover, she went way beyond copying instructions given by the teacher who had asked them to replicate the model cactus displayed in the middle of the table. Our daughter made what she thought to be an ideal cactus. To most people, this was no piece of art, but to me it was the best cactus I had ever seen!

This incident exemplifies two different ways of thinking long recognized by Psychologists. Most people think "reproductively" while a small segment of the population think "productively." With productive thinking, people generate as many alternatives as they can, while reproductive thinking fosters rigidity of thought resulting in copycat behavior.

Unfortunately, many teachers would react like this Botany teacher. They have no idea on how to handle or respond to children who think differently. They often start labeling them as "having something wrong with them." At age six, after a six-month trial at a private school, we felt we had no other choice but to homeschool our daughter. In his book *The Einstein Syndrome*, Sowell describes how "these children are labeled 'hyperactive, or attention deficit disorder,' when in fact they are simply bored by the low level of school work." He goes on to say that "unfortunately, there is much more readiness to medicate such children than to give them more challenging work that would engage their abilities."

I truly believe that all children are born with a capacity for brilliance, and as such, brilliant children should be the norm not the exception. Parents and educators should have greater faith in the learning potential of children, and should stop thinking that average is where everyone should be. This begs the question as to why so many children underachieve and fail to reach their own potential.

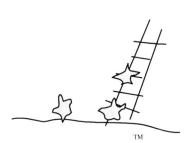

TM

RECAP

FACTS ABOUT BABIES

ALL learning is fun and easy for babies!

ALL babies are eager to learn!

FACTS ABOUT LANGUAGES

1. Language development occurs naturally in a timely fashion.

2. All babies learn to speak without knowing the alphabet or knowing that a word is a noun or a verb.

3. All babies can learn to communicate in sign language as early as 6 months.

35

4. Language is music and each language has its own melody and rhythm.

5. Young children can learn several languages at the same time, without getting confused, because each language has its own song.

6. The teaching of a foreign language in high school or college is unnatural and counterproductive.

7. The best time to expose children to a second language is during the pre-verbal stage because the younger they are the easier it is for them to learn.

8. All babies learn very fast and they forget just as fast, thus the importance of keeping up with the language is evident.

9. Learning a foreign language helps develop respect and tolerance for other cultures.

10. Exposure to multiple languages contributes to higher IQ.

HOW BABIES LEARN ANY LANGUAGE

1. They learn through association and repetition.

2. They learn to recognize sound patterns as a group, such as "Thereisdaddy." "Whereisthecat?"

3. Their brains sort out these sound patterns and break them down into their components.

4. Their brain has the ability to deduce grammar.

5. They learn any language they are exposed to at the unconscious level.

FACTS ABOUT READING

1. ALL babies are born to read just as ALL babies are born to speak their native language.

2. Learning the alphabet or phonics is not necessary in order to learn how to read.

3. Learning to recognize whole words rather than learning phonics is a method best suited for babies.

4. Learning to read is easier for babies than learning to talk because it requires less physical effort.

5. ALL children love stories - by association, reading is a fun activity for children.

6. Developing a love for reading is paramount to the approach of teaching babies to read.

7. Early reading contributes to higher IQ.

TM

HOW TO DEVELOP A LOVE OF READING
IN YOUR BABY

Teaching your baby to read is good, but giving your baby a love of reading is even more important. I want to stress that the use of flashcards and the use of labels are excellent because it gives the child the idea that words stand for things and thoughts. It is easy for the baby to associate the printed word with a sound. However, flashcards and labels are only a start because books should take center stage. Coupled with the exposure to flashcards and labels (objects labeled throughout the house), reading stories every day is essential in order for your child to develop a love for reading. <u>This</u> is the goal - **developing a love for reading**.

I have met some brilliant children who were raised on flashcards of all sorts to give the child "Encyclopedic Knowledge." These children learned "facts" from flashcards that were presented to them. Imagine a 3 year old knowing about type of architecture and period of history! The sad thing is, I never saw them pick up a book by themselves because they were just waiting to be intellectually spoon-fed. So, I cannot stress enough the importance of developing a love for reading stories. Only then will the child **want** to read because reading stories is fun.

To save time, you may want to acquire our flashcards and labels:

Reading Kit by Imagic
Reading And Language Kit by Imagic – English/Spanish
Reading And Language Kit by Imagic – English/French
English Labels by Imagic
Spanish Labels by Imagic
French Labels by Imagic

HOW TO MAKE YOUR OWN FLASHCARDS

Materials used at birth
Purchase some poster board from an office supply store. Make a few large flashcards with lettering at 2 to 3 inches in height using a red marker. The reason for the large print is that at birth, babies cannot focus well. Use all lower case lettering and print as uniformly as you can. Write the name of your baby, , mommy, daddy, and the names of your pets.

Materials used at 3 weeks old
Within a few weeks, your baby will be able to focus on words written in smaller format - about 1 inch in height. Write single words and phrases. See the list on the following pages along with the sample at the back of the book.

As a suggestion, write the corresponding word in the foreign language of your choice on the back of the card using a different color marker. If you choose red for English on one side, choose blue for French or green for Spanish.

Vocabulary suggestions:

SAMPLE WORDS

knee	mommy
belly	daddy
one foot	brother
two feet	sister
ear	a doll
head	a car
nose	cat
little nose	dog
toes	nice cat
little toes	nice dog
tongue	good dog
teeth	teddy bear
elbow	a nice teddy bear
lips	toys
shoulder	animals
mouth	many animals
thumb	baby
one eye	nice baby
two eyes	where is the baby
hand	where is mommy?
two hands	where is daddy?
hair	there is mommy
arm	there is daddy
finger	good-bye
leg	good morning
belly button	good night

big hand	kiss
small hand	many kisses
bathroom	kiss me
diaper	kissing
a bubble	love
bubbles	I love you
some soap	bedroom
bath	pajamas
kitchen	sleep
baby bottle	sweet dreams
milk	light
cookie	night light
water	bed
drinking water	blanket
please	boy
thank you	little boy
refrigerator	girl
table	little girl
chair	the boy is washing
the chair	the girl is laughing
the spoon	the boy is sitting
little spoon	mommy is walking
big spoon	daddy is reading
cup	the dog is jumping
small cup	the cat is running
water in the cup	mommy is dancing
plate	daddy is standing
small plate	ball
spoon on the plate	small ball
glass	big ball
orange	pants

How to play with (use) the flash cards with your baby

For the first 4 to 6 weeks, select only single words from the list, then introduce phrases every other day.

Stop all background noise, i.e. the television, but soft music is ok. Choose a time when you and your baby are rested, comfortable, and not hungry.

Twice a day, lay your baby on the bed or on the carpet and show the flashcards to him and enunciate the word clearly and joyfully. Start the first card by saying "That says mommy/ daddy/ fido/ spot" spending no more than one second between each word. Your smiling attitude and your enthusiasm is a must. When you show body part words, playfully touch that part of his body as you show the card. After about 20 words – it is time for a 1-minute break. Pick him up, give him a kiss, and say joyfully "reading is fun, isn't it?" Vary your show of enthusiasm with a few dance steps or whatever is your style. Observe him when you flash the cards. If he looses interest after 15 words, next time around, stop after 12 words and give him a little break.

MAKING YOUR OWN LABELS

Materials used

In addition to these flashcards, your child can learn to read by association. Label things around the house using 3x5 cards. These cards should be written in lower case format 1/2" to 3/4" high, written as evenly as possible, preferably using a color marker. Tape cards all over the house to label objects - table, chair, refrigerator, etc. It may be several months before your baby can focus on these small cards, but they will be in place when he is able to read them. Several times a week, while your baby is in your arms, give him a tour of the house and pause in front of each card and tell him what it says. Your baby will associate the writing with the object it is taped to. Think of it as fun and your baby will too.

Give your child a tour of the house

As you go around the house on a "labeling tour," tell him, that says "door," and that says "refrigerator." Once in a great while, and only for a few cards, point with your finger to each letter and spell "d" "o" "o" "r." Remember, everything you say must be said joyfully. Do it quickly, do not stay on one card for long. Babies are very quick to pick up meaning and the last thing you want to do is bore him. You are not there to teach him the alphabet because we do not talk or read in alphabet. Letters will only be useful to him much later when he will learn to write. Bear in mind that he will pick up his cues from you. If you think it's fun, he'll think it's fun too.

DEVELOPING A LOVE OF READING IN YOUR BABY

Studies have shown that learning begins while in the womb. In the book *How Babies Talk*, Golinkoff et al report that fetuses can learn to differentiate between different languages, different music and even what is being read to them. Once the babies were born, they were able to recognize their favorite piece of music or their favorite rhyme as measured by an increase in heart rate.

If you did not read to your child during gestation, do start reading to him the first week he is born and read to him every single day. Reading will become a special time for both of you. As you hold him in your arms, read to him while using your finger as a pointer. He will give you his undivided attention because you will become the entertainer as you make the story come alive for him. Naturally, he won't understand a thing at first. But being held with the sound of your voice is soothing and comforting to him, and most of all, you will be developing a ritual with you, him and the book. As you entertain him by reading stories, the book will become a source of entertainment and thus, he will develop a love for reading.

Some suggestions:

- Emphasize the fact that you are "reading a story" rather than "reading a book."

- Heighten his desire to read a story by first spending some time on the cover of the book. Open the book and look at all the pictures and start raising questions as to what could have happened. I guarantee that your child will be dying for you to start reading.

- Make the story exciting by reading the story with inflection in your voice, make it dramatic!

- You can build your baby's own library for very little money by acquiring books at garage sales or at second hand bookstores. Many public libraries have a bookstore where they sell used books for very little money. Besides having his own books that you both read over again, go to the library with him every week and borrow some books. The trip to the library will become familiar to him and it will become a time of excitement at the thought of having new stories to read.

- Teach your baby the excitement of turning pages. When your child can sit (somewhat) put a lightweight store catalogue in front of him and show him how to turn the pages. Small mail order catalogues are also great for your baby because they are smaller and like the large catalogues, they are colorful and full of pictures. Giving him catalogues in his first or second month will give him the habit of turning pages and you will not worry about his drooling over the catalogue and messing up the pages. Turning pages and seeing new pictures emerging is a very exciting thing to a baby.

- Do not forget to use your finger as a pointer because after a while your child will start following your finger and be looking at each word. As the same words will invariably reoccur throughout the book, your child will increase his vocabulary by simple association and repetition.

- After you are aware that your baby's eyes have been following your finger for a while, try to devise a game after reading a book. If the book mentioned some words several times, like "train" or "boat," or whatever subject, select one word and say: "This says **train**." can you point where else we can find the word "train" on this page? If he cannot, do the game yourself. Take his little finger and help him point to the words and say slowly and joyfully "train," "train," "train." One day, when he is ready, he will start to do it by himself. Pick a few words from that book and that is all. Do not bore him.

DEVELOPING THE CREATIVITY IN YOUR BABY

Invent a story - When your baby starts talking, make up some stories with him. Ask him what setting and characters he would like to have in the story. Be prepared to change your plot if it is not satisfactory to him. Don't worry; he will let you know how you are doing. As he grows older, take turns in making up the story - he says one sentence and you say the next.

Do not be too tidy. Give the story a chance to develop. When your child is a little older and he starts playing by himself, let him continue to act out his story where he left off the day before. It is a good idea to ask him every night to put away some of his toys, like a ball, that do not require a "background setting." But, if he has put some characters in an imaginary forest or castle, let the makeshift castle stand as well as leaving the little people where they are. Please don't touch the bridge (the ruler) held in mid air by two chairs. How else could the little people cross the river full of alligators?

TM

HOW TO ENCOURAGE YOUR BABY TO SPEAK
A FOREIGN LANGUAGE

You will be surprised to know that this encouragement is more directed to the parents than the child because it is the parents' determination and consistency that will help the child respond in one language or another.

I want to encourage parents who speak another language to speak that "foreign" language in the home. If only one parent is fluent in another language, then that parent has the duty to pass on his language to the child. I guarantee that your child will be forever grateful to you. That parent needs to make a consistent and conscious effort to speak to the baby in Spanish, French, or other language, <u>as soon as the baby is born</u>. It will take great effort from that parent, but unless he is vigilant about it, the baby will not make the effort either. The baby will learn to speak to the parent in the language he was spoken to by that parent. Responding will be easy. If you are consistent, and you say "Bonjour!" there is no way your child will reply "Good morning!" Answering in that language will be instinctive. If your child needs a little prompting, just repeat "Bonjour!" and he will repeat. Do not push or insist,

REWARD by praising your child when he answers correctly. If you want your child to speak Spanish and he asks for water, just say "agua?" If he says "water" again, repeat "agua?" then give him a glass of water after he said the word correctly.

Some people may want to discourage parents to speaking a foreign language to their children for fear that the baby will not learn to speak the language spoken in this country. I want to reassure parents that the baby will have no problem learning both languages at the same time. In a research paper published in *Language Learning* in December of 1994, "Patterns of Interaction in the Lexical Growth in Two Languages of Bilingual Infants and Toddlers," Barbara Zurer Pearson and Silvia Fernandez found similarity in the rate and pace of development of bilingual or monolingual children."

If neither parent is fluent in a foreign language, I suggest that parents hire a babysitter who is fluent in the language you want your child to learn. Ask the babysitter to only speak her language while she plays, reads, and talks to your baby. Show your appreciation to the babysitter by telling her how much you appreciate her efforts in speaking her language to your child. Do remind your babysitter to be consistent because it is very easy to revert to the English language. If you are a parent who stays home, I suggest that you too learn from the babysitter. Repeat words after the baby sitter and you will be able to reinforce the words with your child after the babysitter leaves. Read a baby book in a foreign language while the babysitter is in your home, and ask her to correct you. Then after she leaves, read it to your baby. Do not worry if you do not have the right accent or pronunciation, your baby knows what you are saying.

Using flash cards and labels in a foreign language will help him learn to read the language as well. Getting books in that foreign language is essential. The keys to teach a foreign language to your baby is CONSISTENCY, REPETITION and PERSEVERANCE.

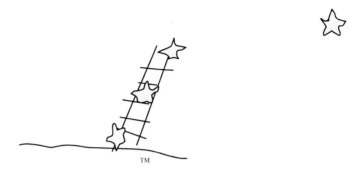

HOW TO UNDERSTAND YOUR BABY'S NEEDS

If you are a first time parent, know that parents learn their duties "on-the-job." However, it is nice to have a few pointers so as to avoid the mistakes of those who went before you. No one pretends to have answers to everything, but there are things that tend to work better than others. We have all made some mistakes in child rearing, and you will too. It is comforting to remind ourselves that "nobody's perfect" and we do the best we can. Parents who have several children have received much training and invariably, they've learned to improve their child rearing techniques with each child.

Your baby is a little person with great physical limitations who has needs that go well beyond feeding and diaper changes. He can't do things for himself and he can't communicate his needs - whether he is hungry, needs a diaper change, feels too hot or too cold, feels bored, needs a hugging, can't sleep because of noise, and so on. He needs your help. Mind you, he is very much aware of his surroundings but he must depend totally on you, and unless you are attuned to his needs, his only recourse after a little moaning is to cry.

Physical needs and limitations - comfort and exercise

Eating, sleeping and being kept clean are essential for his comfort. He will suffer hunger pains if he is not fed on time; he will become irritated if he is prevented from sleeping and if good hygiene is not maintained, he will get a diaper rash. Naturally, it is up to you to cater to his needs. His insatiable desire to explore, learn, and control his environment makes him a budding athlete. He will take every opportunity to develop muscles in his little legs - muscles that will support him when he starts walking. Practicing arm movement and finger dexterity is a must to reach and grab things and play is a perfect medium for exercise.

Psychological needs - love and security

His psychological needs are just as important as his physical needs because it is these needs that will make your baby grow into a confident, well adjusted and loving person.

Is your baby exercising his lungs?

Whoever came up with that idea lacks an understanding of the needs of babies. Simply imagine yourself in a straight jacket and you have messed in your pants and people around you speak Swahili. How can you tell them you are uncomfortable? You first go to step one, moaning, and if after a while they don't get the message, you go to step two, because by now you have diaper rash, and you have no choice but to start crying. Finally after a while they got the message and they changed your diaper. Next time around, you'll try the same thing. However, if people only act upon your crying, then soon you'll put two and two together and think "why waste my energy in step one when I can get a quicker response by jumping to step two." Some children have to cry for a long period of time before getting their needs attended. It is easy to understand how parents can unknowingly shape inappropriate behavior in their children and turn their baby into a "crying baby!"

Some people will say "let him cry, he just wants attention." Wait a minute my dear Watson, he cries for one reason only - his needs are not met and he wants your attention. You have to play Sherlock and figure out what his needs are at that particular time. The worst thing you can do is to ignore the first sign of distress, moaning. A happy baby is one whose needs are met. It's that simple.

TM

HOW TO SET UP POSITIVE HABITS
WITH YOUR BABY AND TODDLER

Your baby will grow very fast and before you know it, he will be a toddler hopping around. It is a good idea to develop good habits early on.

Praise or condemn the behavior, do not attack the personality of the child
Give your child your unconditional love. The choice of words you use is very important when praising or condemning a behavior. When praising your child, use words like "very good!" "You did well!" instead of saying "Good girl!" or "Good boy!" When condemning a behavior, it is also best to follow your comment with an explanation as to why your child should not do a particular behavior. Say "Don't do that <u>because</u> it hurts the cat!" Children are very logical - Giving your child an explanation helps him understand why a particular behavior should or should not be done.

Give the benefit of the doubt and suggest appropriate behavior
Don't say, "You know better than that!" Say instead, "Remember, it hurts the cat when you do that!" and suggest an appropriate behavior, such as

"But, he likes it when you pet him this way!" then show him how. Then reward the behavior when he imitates you with "That's right," "Very nice" or "See, he likes what you are doing!"

Use only positive reinforcement

Reward the behavior you want to produce. You must remember that children like attention and that anytime you give him your attention, this is rewarding to him. Logically, it follows that if he receives more attention when he behaves badly, then he'll behave badly most of the time. The key is to reward good behavior with approval like "That's right," "Very good," "It is nice of you to do that." The use of negative reinforcements such as "you are always a bad boy" or "you'll never learn" will set the stage for self-fulfilling and defeating prophecies, which is quite the opposite of what you want to achieve.

Limits

It is of utmost importance that you set limits for your child. With well-defined limits your child will feel safe and secure. As he grows older he will test those limits and with time you will have to extend them. These restrictions are usually based upon safety factors and every parent knows instinctively what those limits are at each stage of the child's development. If you have to say "no," follow your command with the reasons why he should not be doing something and show him immediately what he can do.

Expectancy

Be realistic and not too demanding in your expectations. Be patient. Remember, that your child is superman in a little body - he does the very best he can physically and mentally. We must appreciate the fact that the rate of learning is related to brain growth. Considering the fact that by age five, the brain is 80% complete, not much learning takes place after that - this should make any adult very humble.

Most children start verbalizing one word at a time. Others don't seem to follow this pattern and wait until they know many words to start talking. Remember Einstein was a late talker. Sometimes, children will talk utter gibberish in complete sentences and whole paragraphs. Then, one day, they talk in perfectly understandable sentences. It is not uncommon for children brought up with several languages to start talking a little later in both languages. However, don't stop reinforcing the second language just because your neighbor's child starts talking and your child isn't. It may be a matter of a few months but have confidence in him. Be assured that your child takes everything in and he rehearses silently for now.

Consistency

Consistency will make things easier for your child. If you are consistent in your expectations, the child will know exactly what you expect of him and he will act accordingly. If you expect him to speak in a foreign language when you start talking to him in a foreign language, respond only when he utters words in the foreign language. You might want to prompt him in the foreign language to let him know that it is the proper way of answering. Never show your disappointment if he does not answer right away. Encourage and reward.

Patience

Have the patience of an oak! Remember that your child has an insatiable desire to please but he can do only what he is physically able to do. Be especially patient in toilet training, remind yourself that it takes time. Praise any small progress.

Do not compare him to another child or a sibling

Each child is different and each child will do what he can do when he is ready. He is a little person who will perform according to his own timing - when he is "good and ready." Moreover, if he cannot draw a circle while his brother could at his age, do not downgrade him. He undoubtedly has other interests or talents. Praise <u>his</u> achievements.

Each child is different

Genetics and environment are two factors that make your child what he is and what he will become. The amount contributed by each depends upon whether you are a naturist - belief in greater contribution of genetics, or a nurturist - belief in the effect of environment factors. I personally believe that environment plays a great part in making children who they are. You can influence his taste by exposing him to what you might consider exciting things, like drawing or painting, but if drawing does not interest him, there is nothing you can do.

However, as a rule, a child will "know" what he is exposed to and he will develop a liking for it. A child who is brought up by artistic parents who paint and draw all the time will undoubtedly develop a liking for these activities. A child of a professional musician will undoubtedly develop a liking for playing a musical instrument. If a lot of reading is done at home, the child will develop a liking for books. Having a variety of toys and books available for him may help him define his interests and talents. Do not say "He'll be a race car driver when he grows up" just because he likes playing with cars, or "He'll be a scientist" just because he likes to look at things under the microscope. Let your child explore and learn about the world around him. Most children in middle or high school do not have a clue of what they want to do "when they grow up," yet in time, usually in college, they are able to go into a relatively narrow field of interest.

Develop some (good) habits
At first, forming habits takes some doing but once the routine is taken, the habit of reading stories every night becomes a daily routine that is anticipated with joy by both parent and child.

Practice makes perfect
Your child has an innate desire to practice anything and everything. Do not interfere with his practice.

Do not talk "baby talk"
Your child is perfectly capable of learning the word "dog" instead of "doggie" and you must encourage him to talk normally. He will pick up his vocabulary from you, and you will guide his sentence structure and choice of words. A child can be told that a crystal, which gives all the colors of the rainbow, is also called a "prism" without putting an academic burden on the child. For children, everything is made easy, it is adults who may "think" that certain things would be hard for a child to learn, and they unknowingly do the child a disservice. By giving your baby a rich vocabulary, he will have a head

start on understanding concepts and have a deeper understanding of the world around him.

Do not pass on your fears or hang-ups to your child

If creepy crawlies are not your thing, don't pass on your fear to your child. Comment positively about them. Let him explore, discover and develop a sense of appreciation with nature. Let him pick up those bugs or frogs or lizards that you can't touch yourself. <u>Believe me,</u> I pride myself on this self-control. To this day I can't hold a frog or a toad that my daughter has picked up.

Terrible twos

Many people will tell you to brace yourself for this stage. Is this perception real? This is the stage when, we are told, children's self-identity develops. "I am Johnny, and I can walk and fetch and do things for myself, and if I don't want to do something, I won't." I personally feel that if your child's needs have been met all along and you've told him why certain things should not be done, he will continue to accept your logical explanation. If, after you have given him a logical explanation, your child wants to try something anyway, let him, as long as he will not physically hurt himself. The reason being that it is important for him to experience the consequences of his actions. If you are too adamant in preventing him from doing something, you will unintentionally increase its appeal.

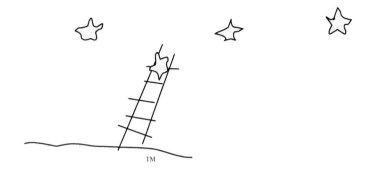

HOW TO HELP YOUR BABY
DEVELOP GOOD MENTAL HEALTH

Talk and listen to your baby

Your baby is a little person who needs your guidance. Help him develop good mental health by helping him understand his feelings and emotions and choosing an appropriate response.

Once he starts talking, listen to him and have conversations with him. Your listening will show him how much you care about him and how much you value his opinions. Also, this will help him develop confidence and gain a good self-concept. He will then share all his experiences with you - happy or sad. Listening will help develop a sense of security and he will come to you for help in solving his little problems. Remember, if you are there for his little problems now, he will also come to you during his teenage years with his (bigger) problems. Be his friend and confidant.

When he comes to you for help, encourage him to think how the problem could be solved and give him some control by asking him "What do you think?" or "What do you think you should do?" or "What are your options?" Show him how much you understand his feelings. You may need to help him put his feelings into words so that he can express himself, like "I bet you must feel frustrated." or "I am sure you must be sad." or feeling angry or jealous, etc. Show him that his feelings or emotions are normal by saying "I know how you must feel, I would probably feel the same way." Ask him "Do you want my opinion?" Be objective and, if needs be, help him put some perspective into a situation by saying, "Do you think you might be over reacting?" Show him that his entire range of emotions is normal.

We all make mistakes

We are all humans, let your child know that you too can make mistakes, and if you do, apologize. If you over-reacted to something he did, just say "I am sorry, I over-reacted, please forgive me." If you over-reacted with your spouse and your child was present, apologize to your spouse in front of your child. This will teach him that it is O.K. to make mistakes but it is important that the mistake be corrected. Kissing to make up helps heal the wounds.

Develop a good sense of humor in your baby

Laugh at yourself - be indulgent with yourself and laugh at stupid errors you may make. Kidding with your child is healthy and is a way to laugh at ourselves. However, do not ridicule or put down your child for any reason. We can laugh at ourselves for stupid things we do. However, ridiculing and putting-down your child attacks his personality which will hurt his self-concept.

Encourage decision-making

Help your child take risks and make decisions for himself. If the outcome turned out great, praise him, if it did not, say "It was worth trying, you've learned a lot." and "Now that you know that, how do you think you would handle this in the future?" or "In the future, what would you do differently?" Praise any little achievement - it is important that he feels good about himself. His confidence will grow with each success and he will gain the confidence to take on more responsibilities as he gets older.

Be fair

Children have a great sense of fairness. Be fair and you will have their respect. The punishment should fit the circumstances, and excessive punishment will have an adverse effect in making the child bitter and resentful. Giving another chance is usually best without resorting to punishment, such as withdrawing privileges. Talk to your child. Fairness is the game!

The pitfall of being a perfectionist

Many bright children will under perform at school because they cannot tolerate failing or making a mistake. It should be understood that often these values came from their parents who are unable to tolerate any mistakes or poor performance.

I have personally known some extremely bright children who were failing in school because of that problem. Some bright children are pressured by their parents to excel in all areas. They may feel that if their children are talented in English and art, then they should also be talented in math and science. Soon, rather than taking the risk of making mistakes, some children will avoid doing the work and pretend they do not understand the material or they will give excuses that they "forgot" to do an assignment. In their minds, if they don't do the work, they have not made any mistakes and consequently they have not "failed." Doing this preserves their self-concept.

Sometimes these perfectionist values are self-imposed. Having many talents means that the child is bright and he knows it. However, because of this fact, he may feel that he should be excelling in everything. I remember that when our little girl was 7 years old, she became devastated by the fact that she could not draw well or ride a bicycle like her friends. She had many talents and was way ahead of her peers, but she saw those two things as handicaps that she would never overcome. We had removed her training wheels because she wanted to be like her friends - but she had convinced herself that she could not bicycle either, like drawing. I told her that God gave her many talents and she should be glad of that, and that she should let some other children have some other talents like drawing. I told her that in the case of riding a bicycle that it was just a matter of determination.

It was a Sunday. I decided that this was the day she was going to learn and we would go to a nearby parking lot for her to practice and we would come back only after she learned how to ride. Ninety minutes later she rode her bicycle home by herself, beaming because <u>she</u> had mastered the first big hurdle of her life!

HAVE FUN WITH YOUR BABY !!

Time is precious and passes too quickly. Enjoy your time with your baby. Being a parent is a very rewarding experience. You will be teaching him many things, in turn he will make you see the world as you have never seen it before. This is the time when you will stop and truly smell the roses and share with him the excitement of seeing a bug walking on a wire or a mother spider carrying her babies on her back. Take a chair and watch with your child how a spider weaves her web, or marvel at the morning dew that accumulated on the web. Freeze this instant in your mind for later delight when your child is all grown up and you can still remember this magical moment.